# SEX MANUAL
# FOR PEOPLE OVER
# 30

*Written by Ira Alterman*
*Designed and Illustrated by Martin Riskin*

AN **Ivory Tower** BOOK

CONTEMPORARY
**BOOKS, INC.**
CHICAGO

Published by arrangement with Ivory Tower
    Publishing Company, Inc.
by Contemporary Books, Inc.
180 North Michigan Avenue, Chicago, Illinois 60601
Manufactured in the United States of America
International Standard Book Number: 0-8092-5354-2

# SEX MANUAL
## FOR PEOPLE OVER
# 30

# INTRODUCTION

The difference between sex after 30 and sex before 30 is the difference between fine wine and soda pop. It's the difference between a Ph.D. and a high school diploma, between the tango and the boogaloo, between prime rib and hamburger, between the big leagues and the bush leagues, between flying first class and taking the bus.

Sex after 30 is a symphony orchestra; sex before 30 is playing the spoons.
Sex after 30 is a tailored tuxedo; sex before 30 is a t-shirt and jeans.

Sex after 30 is a jog in the park; sex before 30 is the 100 yard dash.

Sex after 30 is art, form, and style; sex before 30 is lunge, grab, and tear.

Sex after 30 is a suite at the Plaza; sex before 30 is the back seat of a Dodge.

# HOW
# TO
# TELL
# IF
# YOU'VE
# LOST
# IT

People who have passed the age of 30 sometimes forget to bring something with them on their journey out of their twenties. It is called their sex drive. Whereas many could at one time boast, "Once is never enough for me," now, frequently, once is too much.

Has that happened to you? Is your sex drive in reverse? Has the engine that drives a once voracious sexual appetite sputtered, coughed, burped, backfired and died?

Have you lost your sex drive, or only misplaced it? Not certain? Then you should take the following test.

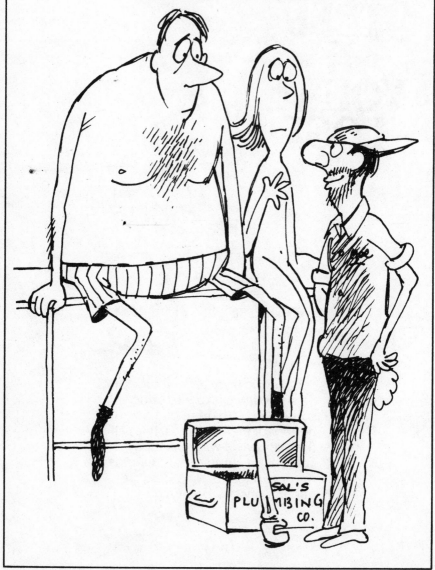

# THE FOLLOWING TEST

The following test will help you clear up the status of your sex drive. Choose what seems to be the appropriate answer:

## 1. If I had to select one of the following books to read in bed at night, I would pick:

| |
|---|
| a. U.N. Orgy |
| b. The History of Lint |
| c. I Married My Goat |

## 2. Faced with a choice of an evening out, I would want to go to:

| |
|---|
| a. Watch a nude mud wrestling match. |
| b. The library to hear a lecture on beet farming. |
| c. A perverts' rodeo. |

## **3.** Complete the sentence.
## "I get horny...

a. about three times a week."

b. about three times a decade."

c. as soon as I open my eyes in the morning."

## **4.** What would your first reaction be if someone said to you,
## "Fish don't have orgasms?"

a. Thank god I'm not a fish.

b. I wonder if I am a fish?

c. That's because fish have never met me.

**5.** If I felt someone brushing intimately against me on a crowded subway, my first reaction would be to:

a. First make sure they weren't ugly, then brush back.

b. Rearrange their face with my elbow.

c. Beg for a cavity search.

**6.** For me, the most pleasant thing about sex is:

a. The quiet delirium of a good multiple orgasm.

b. When it's finally over.

c. Putting unguent on the whip marks.

# Rate your Answers:

Question #1 (also questions 2, 3, 4, 5, and 6): If you answered "a" then you haven't lost it; you have a healthy sex drive. If you answered "b" then you have lost it; you have no sex drive. If you answered "c" you not only have your own healthy sex drive, you have the sex drive lost by the guy who answered "b".

# REDISCOVERING FOREPLAY

*A high foreplay quotient means you have a very high degree of interest in foreplay.*

This is all about you and your foreplay quotient. A foreplay quotient refers to the degree of interest you have in foreplay. For example, a high foreplay quotient ("10" on a scale of 10) means you have a very high degree of interest in foreplay. A low foreplay quotient ("1" on a scale of 10) means you have a very low degree of interest in foreplay (sailors who have been at sea for a long time and rapists fall into this category).

Rate your own foreplay quotient, then see how you compare to the rest of those who are over 30 ( "6" is the average foreplay quotient for over-30's).

# Rating Your Own Foreplay Quotient

Rating your own foreplay quotient is easy. Just fill in the blanks as honestly as you can, selecting your answers from the designated lists. Then have your sex partner read your answers and rate you on a scale of 1 (low) to 10 (high).

When it comes to making love, I like to _____.
*(select answer from column A)*

The first thing I do is _____.
*(select answer from column B)*

I think it is probably correct to say that all of the poeple I have ever made love to have gone away _____.
*(select answer from column C)*

I have a technique that works best when I _____.
*(select answer from column A)*

It is based on my tendency to _____.
*(select answer from column B)*

After I have been with them, my lovers always leave _____.
*(select answer from column C)*

## Column A

**1.** really take my time.
**2.** get it over with as soon as possible.
**3.** keep all my clothes on.
**4.** pretend my partner is someone else.
**5.** close my eyes and lie very still until it is all over.
**6.** grunt like a goat.
**7.** skip all the romantic baloney and go right to work.

## Column B

**1.** get my partner excited in any way I can.
**2.** have a quick orgasm and go to sleep.
**3.** check the bed for bugs.
**4.** find something to complain about.
**5.** brace myself for the pain that is sure to follow.
**6.** turn on the television so I won't be bored.
**7.** get into one position and stay there.

## Column C

**1.** very, very happy.
**2.** and never come back.
**3.** complaining about what I did to them with my tongue.
**4.** to find a policeman.
**5.** vowing to get revenge.
**6.** glad they were able to escape.
**7.** feeling dirty and used.

# HOW TO PACE YOURSELF

Sometimes when people who are over 30 go at each other with the pent up sexual fury of two savage animals, the experience lasts for 18 seconds before they start panting like blowfish and begging for oxygen. This is because they have not paced themselves.

Pacing yourself in your sexual performance is important as you get older. It helps prolong the experience and keeps you from gagging on your own sweat.

"Well," some people ask, "how do I know if I'm not pacing myself?" This is an easy question to answer. You are not pacing yourself if your partner has climbed the mountain of fulfillment and you are still putting on your hiking boots.

You are not pacing yourself if you are ready to move on from foreplay and your partner has already showered, changed into flannel pajamas, and fallen asleep.

You are not pacing yourself if your partner keeps prying open your mouth to make sure you have not swallowed your tongue.

"Well," some people ask, "how do I pace myself?" No problem. There are three easy methods to choose from.

# 3 EASY METHODS TO CHOOSE FROM

**1.** The "Watch A Few Minutes Of The Tonight Show In Between Positions" Method.

**2.** The "Hey, Why Don't We Make Love In Slow Motion" Method.

**3.** The "Just Because I Keep Falling Asleep Doesn't Mean I Don't Love You" Method.

# ORGASMS AFTER 30

# HOW TO MAKE THEM BETTER

Experts agree that there are three types of orgasms experienced by people over 30.

The first is characterized by pronounced lethargy and a tendency to fall asleep while the other person is still struggling to be fulfilled.

# ORGASMS AFTER 30
## How To Make Them Better

The second is accompanied by a high-pitched, reedy wail, an excess of thrashing, and deep and penetrating sobs of gratitude. The third, and most common type, occurs from 3 to 11 seconds after the start of intercourse and belies a sex life as rich and varied as that of a sponge.

# ORGASMS AFTER 30
## How To Make Them Better

Not surprisingly, many people over 30 are dissatisfied with the quality of their orgasms and want to make them better (as opposed to those who are dissatisfied with the quantity of their orgasms and just want to have more of them). Like learning to play the piano, this is largely a matter of practice, practice, practice.

Of course, it is also a matter of technique.

# A MATTER OF TECHNIQUE

There are many, many techniques which people over 30 can use to improve the quality of their orgasms. Some are good for some people, some are good for others. You choose for yourself, because when it comes to getting a better orgasm, you can always:

**1.** Strap blenders on your hips and set the controls for "grind."

**2.** Plug yourself into a milking machine.

**3.** Conjure up an image of the simultaneous flushing of a thousand mink lined toilets.

**4.** Say to yourself, "I don't care if it is prematuare ejaculation. This time I'm not holding anything back."

# COMMON OVER-30 SEX FEARS AND HOW TO FIGHT THEM

You would think that by the time people were 30, all of their sex fears would have been worked out. But this is not so. Age adds to, not diminishes, many fears about sex. And fear causes tension, and tension causes you to be frigid, and being frigid causes you to lose your partner to someone who is under 30. I mean, who wants to make love to a tense, frigid, old person. I don't blame your partner. But here's how to get your partner back. Here's how to fight those common over-30 sex fears.

# How To Fight Those Common Over-30 Sex Fears

## What The Fear Is

I don't look sexy anymore.

I'm not desirable anymore.

It's been so long, I bet it doesn't work anymore.

I'm not sexy, I'm not desirable, it's been so long, I bet my partner's seeing another person.

## What To Do About It

Make love in the dark.

Invite total strangers into your bedroom, take off your clothes, and say, "Tell me the truth, do you want to have your way with me?" The results will make you more confident.

Try it out with someone else first, just to make sure that it does.

Get yourself a lover and file for divorce.

# GREAT EXCUSES FOR NON-PERFORMANCE

Let's face it; it happens to everybody over 30 (except me). The mood will be right, your partner will be willing (even encouraging), the fireworks will be set to explode, and time will be ready to stand still — and you just won't be able to perform. Not that you don't want to; not that your body won't be screaming with desire. It's just that a certain area of your anatomy located between your navel and your upper thighs will be out to lunch.

*Let's face it; it happens to everybody (except me).*

Usually in this circumstance you will sink back to the bed/sofa/back seat/floor flushed with embarrassment and mumble some lame excuse about "never happened before."

Well, that doesn't need to be the case. You're over 30 now. You have to expect that these moments will arise from time to time. You just need to be prepared for the humiliation.

# How to be prepared for the humiliation

If you are prepared for the humiliation that accompanies non-performance (which is a whipping offense in at least five states and one prominent motel chain) you can sink back to the bed/sofa/back seat/floor flushed with embarrassment and mumble a great excuse. At least you will save some of your dignity. You can always say:

1. "I can't help it. You're like an angel, and making love to you would be like defiling a sacred thing."

# Great Excuses for non-performers

**2.** "I can't help it. I love you too much to give you this disease."

**3.** "I don't understand it. This is the first time this has happened to me today."

# Great Excuses for non-performers

**4.** "Listen, are you sure we're doing the right thing?"

**5.** "I already gave at the office."

# Great Excuses for non-performers

**6.** "Did I tell you that today I'm starting this new diet — no fried foods, no alcohol, no sex?"

**7.** "I'm sorry, but suddenly it doesn't seem so important when you consider the vastness of the universe."

# Great Excuses for non-performers

**8.** "I'm sorry, but suddenly it doesn't seem so important when you consider that we've already made love 8 times."

**9.** "Don't take offense, but I think of you more as a spiritual being."

**10.** "I think I twisted my ankle."

# CREATIVE CHEATING

Sometimes it will happen that people over 30 who have been with another person for a period of time will get the urge to seek out the company of a new person and to have an intimate relationship with this person. Whether this need is the result of an identity crisis, a change of life, an impulse to reaffirm one's sexuality, or being an inconsiderate, double-crossing, egocentric swine is not important. What is important is not getting caught.

# CREATIVE CHEATING

Usually, people who are cheating get caught because they don't use good alibis. They will say things like, "Where was I? Oh, working late at the office."(a really bad excuse if you don't happen to have an office). Or, "Um, uh, traffic was just awful. I've never had the trip take five hours before." (A terrible excuse if you live upstairs from your store.)

These same people who are causing the terrible overcrowding in all the divorce courts would be happy, contented folks if only they knew something about creative cheating.

# Something About Creative Cheating

Creative cheating is a finely honed personal skill whose main goal is to prevent a beloved one from asking, "Where have you been?"

*You can prevent a loved one from asking this by saying any number of things; things like:*

**1.** "Don't wait up for me tonight; I'm going for a ride on a manned space shuttle."

**2.** "Boy, I feel kind of restless today. I think I'll walk to Albuquerque."

**3.** "I really don't want to go on this secret trip, but the boss says I have to. And don't try to reach me through the office, okay? Nobody's supposed to know where I am."

# CREATIVE CHEATING

**4.** "They want me in Washington."

**5.** "I'm going out for a while. I just need to be alone with my thoughts."

# CREATIVE CHEATING

**6.** "I know it's late, but I have an incredible urge for chocolate donuts. I'll just run over to that little all-night bakery way on the other side of town."

**7.** "Honey, I'm calling from Houston. Can't talk now — I've got to catch a plane. I'll explain when I get home."

**8.** "Don't wait up for me. I'm going to have a flat on the way home from work."

# FIVE NEW WAYS TO USE YOUR TONGUE

One of the complaints that people over 30 have about sex is that it can get boring. Same old fetishes, same old kinky sex games, same old cheap thrills. I mean, when you've been through the 483 basic positions, what's left?

The tongue.

"Oh sure," you say, "I know all about French kissing and that stuff. What else could there be?"

Plenty. Take, for example, the Five New Ways to Use Your Tongue.

# THE FIVE NEW WAYS
# TO USE YOUR TONGUE

The five new ways to use your tongue were culled from many thousands of suggestions contributed by orally fixated people from my very own neighborhood. Some of them were colorful, some of them were impractical, some of them were downright impossible. Nonetheless, they were all field tested (and I have the grass stains to prove it) and the best of the bunch are presented here.

*Try any of these, and I guarantee that your sex life will take on new meaning. Try:*

**1.** Using your tongue to coat your partner's body with Bosco.

**2.** Putting a little shoe on your tongue, then tap dancing your way into your partner's heart.

# THE FIVE NEW WAYS
# TO USE YOUR TONGUE

**3.** Pretending that your tongue is a bobsled and that your partner is a bobsled run.

**4.** Pretending that your tongue is a pearl diver and that your partner is an oyster.

**5.** Using your tongue to tie a square knot somewhere on your partner's body.

# 4
# NEVER FAIL TECHNIQUES FOR AROUSING A SLEEPING PARTNER

The urge to have sex doesn't always come as frequently to people over 30 as it did when these people were under 30. That is why it is important to react to every urge to have sex whenever it occurs. I mean, it may be months before it occurs again. (Not my personal problem, of course, but I hear ugly stories.)

# THE 4 NEVER FAIL TECHNIQUES FOR AROUSING A SLEEPING PARTNER

Frequently these urges come to people over 30 in the middle of the night when they are awake thinking about growing old. Trying, as it were, to go with the flow, they reach out for their partner and find the partner asleep. What to do?

# There are two basic approaches:

**1.** Start by yourself and hope your partner (a) wakes up and joins in the fun, or (b) doesn't get so steamed at being awakened that you get cut off for the rest of the year.

**2.** Use one of the 4 never fail techniques for arousing a sleeping partner.

# THE 4 NEVER FAIL TECHNIQUES FOR AROUSING A SLEEPING PARTNER

These four never fail techniques for arousing a sleeping partner are the most promising from among literally hundreds of techniques practiced by sex partners in varying cultures around the world. They are better than "tying your sleeping spouse to the tail of a camel, then hot-wiring the camel's hump," or "prodding your partner where it counts with a super-charged Hoover." See which one works best for you. The next time you get an urge and your partner is sleeping, why don't you try:

# THE 4 NEVER FAIL TECHNIQUES FOR AROUSING A SLEEPING PARTNER

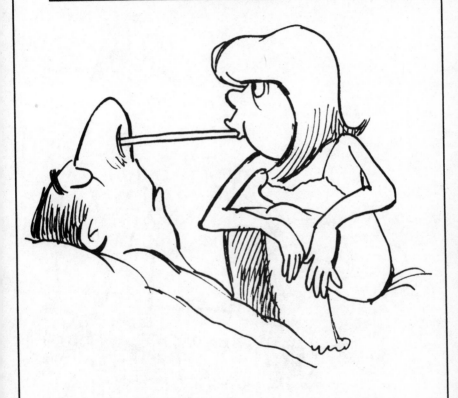

**1.** Inserting a straw into your partner's nostril and blowing up your partner's nose.

**2.** Filling your partner's navel with wild honey, then opening the bedroom window and calling for a bear.

# THE 4 NEVER FAIL TECHNIQUES FOR AROUSING A SLEEPING PARTNER

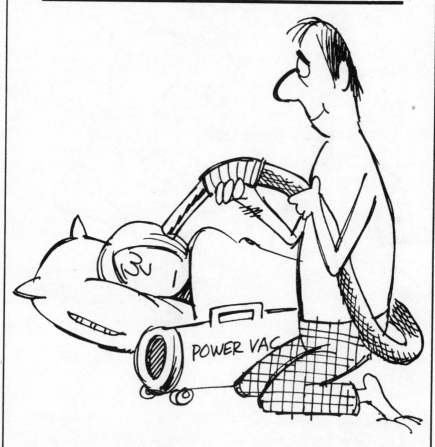

**3.** Putting your lips to your partner's ear and engaging in some intense subliminal whimpering.

**4.** Tying your sleeping spouse to the tail of a camel, and prodding the camel where it counts with a super-charged Hoover.

# 8 EROTIC USES FOR FLAB

Face it. Flab is a fact of life for people over 30. Exercise if you want; diet if you want; wrap your body in a rubber suit and bounce yourself off the walls if you want. You are only delaying the inevitable. Flab follows you into your 30's like winter follows autumn and flies follow mayors.

Hey, let the under 30s make jokes if they want to. They don't know how sexy flab can be.

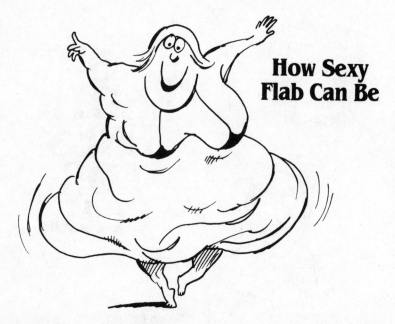

# How Sexy Flab Can Be

Flab can be pretty sexy stuff, if you know what to do with it. Here are 8 erotic ideas.

**1.** Dress yourself in something sexy to wear to bed, and dress your flab in a different sexy thing to wear to bed, presenting the illusion that you are actually two people. Then turn to your partner and say, "Let's have an orgy."

**2.** Put running lights on your flab, then turn to your partner and say, "Control tower to pilot, control tower to pilot. Come on in for a landing."

**3.** Paint your flab so that it looks like a submarine, then pull your partner on board and shout, "Fire one!"

**4.** Pretend that you are Moby Dick, then see if your partner can harpoon you.

**5.** Hide small plastic charges in your flab, then detonate them while you are making love, asking later, "Did the earth move for you, too?"

**6.** Cover your flab with sequins, then turn to your partner and say, "How would you like to make it with the Supremes?"

**7.** Have a replica of the universe tattooed on your flab, then go home, take off your clothes, and say to your partner, "Let's test the Big Bang theory of creation."

**8.** Paste pictures of people making love to your flab, stick your finger in a light socket and become your own pornographic movie.

# SEARCHING FOR YOUR "O" POINT

Some nights people over 30 who are in the mood just can't think of anything new to do.

Boy, is that boring, playing the same old "sex slave in bondage" or "take me in butter" games.

When this is happening to you, why not have your partner help you search for your "O" point.

This is the point on your body that makes you go "Ooooooooohhhhhhhh" whenever your partner touches it.

# SEARCHING FOR YOUR "O" POINT

Sometimes just touching it with a plain old hand or finger or tongue won't do the trick. Sometimes it has to be a hand or finger or tongue coated with olive oil. Sometimes it has to be a hand or finger or tongue that suddenly touches you as you stand trembling with anticipation in a dark room. Sometimes you won't discover your "O" point until your partner touches you with his or her "O" point.

Later, when this gets boring, you can play another searching game. This is called, "Searching for Aiiiyyyeee Alley."

# HOW TO TELL AN ORGASM FROM A HEART ATTACK

The only difference between an orgasm and a heart attack is that after a heart attack, you don't feel like putting a $20 bill on the dresser.

# HOW TO
# TELL AN ORGASM
# FROM A
# HEART ATTACK

The only difference between an orgasm and a heart attack is that a heart attack uses up less kleenexes.

# HOW TO TELL AN ORGASM FROM A HEART ATTACK

The only difference between an orgasm and a heart attack is that after a heart attack, you don't feel like going downstairs and making yourself a cheeseburger.

# HOW TO
# TELL AN ORGASM
# FROM A
# HEART ATTACK

The only difference between an orgasm and a heart attack is that after a heart attack you don't have to go to the bathroom to get cleaned up.

# WHEN IT'S BEEN SO LONG THAT YOU FORGET WHICH ARM IT'S UNDER...

This is a little refresher for those people who are over 30 who might not have had sex since they were under 30 and can't quite remember where all the moving parts are.

## Male Reproductive Organs

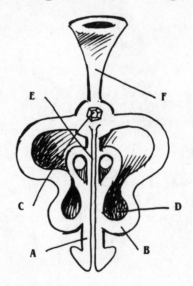

**A.** SNAKE OF LIFE
**B.** VALVE OF RELIEF
**C.** JEWEL PLUM OF NAUGHTY DESIRES
**D.** SACK OF CONTAINMENT
**E.** BOULEVARD OF URGENCY
**F.** HORN OF PLENTY

# Female Reproductive Organs

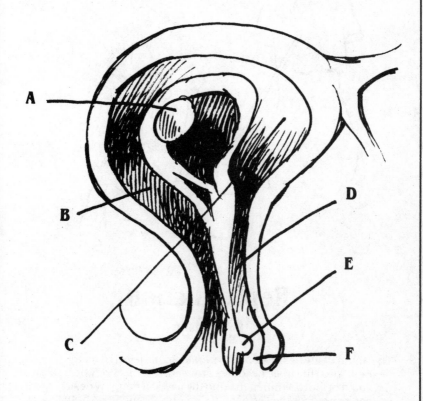

A. THE BASKET OF HIDDEN DANGERS
B. TUBE OF SANCTUARY
C. HALL OF CONCEPTION
D. AVENUE OF RAPTURE
E. DIGIT OF DELIGHT
F. GATE OF FORBIDDEN PLEASURES

# Reproduction Cycle:

The liquid of life lies stored in the male, in his jewel of naughty desires. When the male becomes aroused, internal body heat causes the liquid of life to simmer, making the jewel of naughty desires swell so that it stretches the sac of containment. (Sometimes both jewels swell at the same time, causing a reaction known in medical circles as "letting go with both barrels.") The liquid of life soon starts to boil and the pressure forces it up the boulevard of urgency, down through the snake of life and finally out the valve of relief. If, during this process, the male's snake of life has passed through the female's gate of forbidden pleasures and is buried in the avenue of rapture, the liquid of life spurts deep into the female's hall of conception and trickles into the tube of sanctuary. There, if it is a certain time of the month, the liquid of life will encounter the oval of regret, which is dispensed at given intervals from one of the female's two baskets of hidden dangers.

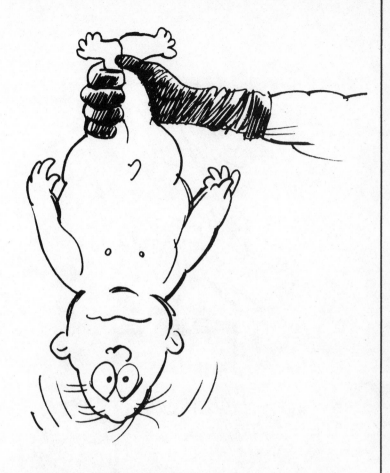

The two separate agents join forces and return to the hall of conception where they are nurtured by natural body juices until, some nine months later, with the hall of conception swollen so that it can no longer contain the growth, a baby is born.

Both the digit of delight, in the female, and the horn of plenty in the male, do not figure in sexual encounter. The horn of plenty is a storage place for excess body fluids and when full releases them directly through the latter part of the boulevard of urgency and out the valve of relief.

No one knows what purpose the digit of delight serves.

Reproduction is like the hives: it's an itch that needs to be scratched. Though most people know how to scratch, few are aware of the intricate cycle that occurs between the time the itch is satisfied and the day they find themselves knee-deep in diapers and brown stuff. It is nature's way of reminding you that there are taxes on the wages of sin.

**What happens is this:** In the basket of hidden danger there is one egg. Nobody knows who puts it there, but many would-be bachelors would like to get their hands on this person. The egg is placed well back in the nest, so it doesn't get a draft when the doors of the nest are opened and closed; otherwise the baby would be born with a stiff neck.

The female then lets the male know she is ready for fertilization. Ads are taken out in newspapers. "There will be a fertilization party at Marcia's Tuesday night. Bring cash." Now it is up to the male. He must gather his seed (called 'getting it up'), plow the soils of life, (called 'getting it in'), and then plant the seed (called 'getting it off').

Of course, it is not as easy as one, two, three. Problems may be encountered at each step. At seed gathering time, for example, the male may be too tired to assemble his seed. It is up to the female to arouse his interest. This is best done in any number of ways: the singing of inspirational songs, reading from the Scriptures, or pretending his fertilizer is a wind instrument and it's time for a clarinet lesson. On the other hand, the male may have problems with step two, plowing the soil. At this time many females like to be told funny stories to put them at ease, stories about love, marriage (if already married, fidelity) and the like.

**Woman's Reproduction Organs:** To get an idea of what the female reproduction organs look like, head on, pretend you are looking at a moose, head on. The moose's antlers are the fallopian tubes. Tucked inside the curl of the horns are little almond-shaped critters called ovaries, one on each side. Where Bullwinkle's skull ought to be is the uterus, and down below that is the vagina. The opening of the vagina is between the legs (surprise!) and is protected by folds of skin and flesh known as the vulva (named after the famous horde-master, Taurus Vulva, who was the first to discover its whereabouts). Where the inner folds of the vulva meet in front there is a small, sensitive tip called the clitoris, after the Greek goddess Clito, goddess of small talk.

**Man's Reproduction Organs:** To get an idea of what the male reproduction organs look like, check out the man's john in the Greyhoud bus station in Providence, R.I. Or imagine a snake resting between two plums.

**How Babies Are Born:** Babies are born from carelessness. So be careful. Once very 28 days or so, one ovary releases an egg cell, which travels into the tube and waits for the sperm to come, if you'll pardon the expression. The egg plays hard to get. Sometimes a sperm will come to the mouth of the tube and holler, "Is anybody home?" And the egg will say, "No, she went to a movie Harold." The male releases 400 to 500 million sperm, at a time. Some of them get very discouraged by the odds (because only one sperm fertilizes the egg) and hang around, trying to make time with the clitoris. However, one sperm usually gets through to the egg and they have a hell of a time, dancing, singing, going to ball games together and fun things like that.

And now what happens is the baby becomes very lonely. He's got nobody to talk to or to sing with. He says to himself, "I gotta get out of here." But he's very small, so small that the journey from the back of the nest to the front of the nest is to him like going crosstown on foot. Unthinkable. He decides to get some rest first, lean back, take a little nap. The next thing he knows, he wakes up he's seven months old. He panics. "Christ, if I don't get out of here soon, I'm gonna miss kindergarten." Then he discovers he has no muscle coordination and spends the next two months exercising for the trip. At first all he can manage are random kicks and blows with his tiny little fists. Then his kicking and hitting becomes more regular. Soon, he's taking solid, well timed shots at the walls of the nest, which are very swollen from all the abuse. Many people think the nest gets so big to make room for the baby.

Soon, the nest owner gets ticked off. She knows the kid is doing it on purpose and tells him to knock it off. She swears and cries and calls her doctor, who hustles her to the hospital. When the kicking and hitting becomes very regular, like the baby is keeping time to The Flight of The Bumblebee, the doctor knows the baby is ready. He puts the mother on a table and places a M&M at the mouth of the nest. The baby stops hitting when he smells the M&M. (He hasn't had a good meal for nine months.) He reaches for it. As soon as the doctor sees the little hand appear and try to snatch the candy, he grabs it and yanks the baby out of there, and gives him a shot in the ass for being such a bad boy. The baby, meanwhile, realizes he has made a bad mistake and tries to go back into the nest. (Many people spend all of their life trying to go back to the nest.) But it is no good. He is born.

# HOW TO
# HAVE SEX WITH YOUR
# CLOTHES ON

Many people who are over 30 like to have sex with their clothes on. They like to do this because it hides their cellulite. They think that if their sex partners see them without clothes, it will make their sex partners:

☐ turn away in disgust.

☐ loose their lunch, then turn away in disgust.

☐ suddenly remember a previous engagement.

Having sex with your clothes on is okay, as long as you do not overdo it.

# What Is Overdoing It

*You know you are overdoing it if:*

**1.** You say to your partner, "Let me slip into something comfortable" and return in a snowsuit.

**2.** You come to your partner wearing more than one girdle.

**3.** The only thing in your lingerie drawer is a wet suit.

**4.** You say to your partner, "Let me slip into something that's out of this world," and return dressed like an astronaut.

# A LITTLE ADVICE ABOUT UNDERWEAR

Many people who wore sexy underwear when they were under 30 try to continue that practice when they are over 30. Many women who are over 30 still force themselves into bikini underpants, and many men who are over 30 still force themselves into briefs. They think this still makes them look sexy.

They are wrong.

# A Little Advice About Underwear

Many women over 30 who wear bikini underpants
look like six gallons of water poured into a one
pint container. Many men over 30 who still wear
briefs look like mutant boy scouts.

These undergarments do not make people over
30 look sexy. These undergarments make people
over 30 look like irregular pork sausages.

My advice to you? Stop wearing underwear
altogether and start wearing very high socks.

# HOW TO
# KEEP THE KIDS OUT
# OF YOUR BEDROOM

One thing that married people over 30 worry about is that their children will walk in on them when they are having sex.

This causes many married people over 30 not to have sex, or to try to have it in the middle of the night when the kids are sure to be asleep. Unfortunately, in the middle of the night you are likely to be asleep, too.

What can you do? If you lock the bedroom door or push a bureau in front of it to keep the kids out, they will know something is going on and stand outside your bedroom and whimper until you get up and let them in. Or they will go back to their own rooms with deep-seated emotional problems and run up big bills with a child psychologist.

# How can you solve this problem and keep the kids out of your sex life? There are 2 ways.

## Two Ways To Keep The Kids Out of Your Sex Life

**1.** Wait until the kids are asleep, then go into the garage and have sex in the car.

**2.** Wait until kids grow up and move out of the house.

Believe me, nothing else works.

# KISSING AFTER 30

Kissers over 30 can be divided into four categories:

## 1. Avoiders
## 2. Peckers
## 3. Cold Fish
## 4. Goldfish

**Avoiders** are people who pretend to want to kiss you, then turn away at the last second so that your lips merely brush their cheek as you lose your balance and plummet to the floor. Many people dislocate their lips trying to kiss avoiders, a feat which can be accomplished only by first lodging the face of the avoider under a heavy object, such as a piano, sofa, or Lincoln Continental.

**Peckers** kiss like chickens. Kissing a pecker is like sending Morse code — and the message is "this is boring." Many of your peckers have a pathological fear of catching a terrible disease, or are just plain frigid. Kissing a pecker is about as satisfying as kissing a hubcap. Many people who start out as goldfish evolve into peckers soon after marriage.

**Cold Fish** are like peckers with staying power. They like to kiss by first sucking all of the moisture out of their lips, then pressing them firmly together and leaving them pressed. It is impossible to force your tongue into the mouth of a cold fish, who would only bite it if you could. Cold fish will hold a kiss for a long time, if you like. I mean, it's nothing personal.

**Goldfish** kiss like they are trying to see how much of your face they can get into their mouth. This is great fun until it is time for you to breathe. It is a good idea to wear a bib when you are kissing a goldfish. Many people who kiss goldfish have to visit chiropractors to get their jaws re-hinged. Goldfish like to have sex by the second date. Finding a goldfish is a stroke of good luck.

Rate your own place on the kissing spectrum. When was the last time you thought about kissing, anyway? Maybe this will explain why you have trouble getting dates.

# HOW TO HAVE NEW THRILLS WITH THE SAME OLD PARTNER

Many people over 30 who are still having sex are having it with a person they have been having it with for a long time. This can be boring. People who are in this situation let their minds wander during sex, thinking about interesting documentaries they have seen on public television, or changing the oil in the Chevy, or whether the tulips need more manure.

This is not a healthy situation. Some people try to alleviate this boredom by imagining they are with a different person, or by making their partner dress up like a virgin, but after a time this also becomes boring. "Holy Toledo," they wonder, "am I ever going to have new thrills with my same old partner?"

Of course. It is just a matter of changing your perspective.

# Changing Your Perspective

If you can't change your partner, you've got to change your perspective. You've got to be willing to try new things. You've got to be willing to:

---

**1.** Change the place you have sex. Bored by your usual positions? See how bored you get running through them on the roof of your house.

---

*Change the place you have sex.*

**2.** Change the time you have sex. Next time, don't wait until the company leaves. Have sex in the kitchen while they are all in the dining room waiting for dessert.

---

**3.** Change the atmosphere in which you have sex. It is a proven fact that oxygen can be boring. The next time you have sex, have it where there is no oxygen, like in a large plastic bag or under water.

---

# 10
## GREAT STEAMY SEX GAMES

Steamy sex games are wonderful in their own right, but what makes them even more wonderful is being able to make up your own rules as you go along.

Below are 10 great steamy sex games you can make even better by making up rules that are particularly well suited for you and your sex partner.

We won't try to inhibit you by describing these games. That's why you have an imagination.

# See what you can make of 10 steamy sex games like:

| | |
|---|---|
| **1.** | Upside-down Rodeo |
| **2.** | Quick, Veronica, My Whip |
| **3.** | The Acrobat and the Chain Gang |
| **4.** | Strangers in the Dark |
| **5.** | Oh, Officer! |
| **6.** | Would You Mind If My Girlfriend Slept Over Tonight? |
| **7.** | Bigger, Harder, Hotter |
| **8.** | Undress Me With Your Teeth |
| **9.** | No, Bogey, No! |
| **10.** | Really Slow Orgasm |

# HOW TO HAVE LAID BACK SEX WITH AN UPTIGHT PARTNER

One night you and your sex partner will be lying abed and you will be overcome by a sudden urge to get into the ancient Laotian Position of the Leaping Pig (the one involving the two hand maidens, the heated benwa balls, and the soy sauce).

You know in your heart of hearts, though, that if you make this suggestion to your partner, who is not too crazy about hand maidens in the first place, a chill will descend over the room and you won't have sex again until Teddy Roosevelt's birthday.

How can you get your uptight partner in the mood? How should I know? What do I look like, Sigmund Freud? If alcohol and persistent begging don't do the trick, roll over onto your own side of the bed and suck your thumb until you fall asleep. That's what I do.

# FAKING IT

Being able to fake orgasms in a convincing way is essential to many over-30 relationships.

People who are under 30 can have orgasms whenever they want to. It has something to do with a high hormone level and the constant friction of tight jeans.

People over 30, though, have quality rather than quantity orgasms. The problem is, they don't always have them at the same time.

If one partner has a great one and the other partner is lying there like a turnip, the first partner frequently feels guilty and sometimes gets angry and always rolls out of bed nursing a bruised ego. This can lead to a sense of inadequacy and a trial separation if it happens too often.

Better you should fake having an orgasm and keep the relationship stable (while you look for someone who can do the job on the side.)

# How To Fake Having an Orgasm

*There are really only three steps to faking orgasm, though there are many embellishments on these steps:*

**1.** When you sense your partner is about to have an orgasm (finally), shout/whisper/moan words of encouragement ("Yes, yes, yes," or "I'm ready, I'm ready," or "Take me, take me, take me.") You may have your own favorite words of encouragement. Note that repetition is important. Hearing your eager, lust-filled voice will take your partner's attention away from the fact that you have been lying there like a dead halibut.

**2.** When your partner starts to have the orgasm, tense your body as though you are having one, too. Use your nails, use your teeth, flail your head from side to side. Pretend you have just touched a high voltage wire. Knock over a lamp. Get your partner into a bear hug. Go ape.

**3.** Scream (high and piercing, low and moaning, short and staccato, long and loud) and go limp (perspire if you can).

The trick is to make your partner think the experience was wonderful, but not to be so convincing that your partner wants to take another whack.

# SOPHISTICATED POSITIONS THAT YOUNG LOVERS DON'T HAVE THE PATIENCE TO PRACTICE

One advantage to being over 30 (and so far it's the only one I can think of) is that you're not in as much of a hurry to do things as when you were under 30.

This certainly extends to lovemaking. Over-30s are more willing to be patient. This, in turn, can lead to fuller, more satisfying sex.

## How To Have Fuller, More Satisfying Sex

Having fuller, more satisfying sex is easy as long as you have the patience to practice sophisticated positions. I'm talking about positions like:

**1. Side-by-Side** — You and your sex partner lie side by side in the nude until an earthquake throws one of you on top of the other one so you can make whoopie.

**2. Ice Is Nice** — You and your sex partner have your bodies encased in separate blocks of ice with only your heads free, lie on each other, then blow each other's block off.

**3. Breathless** — You and your sex partner disrobe and stand at opposite corners of a small room, then try to get together by inhaling as deeply as possible and sucking each other across the room.

# TEST YOUR SEX IQ

## Answer true or false:

Men who wear dresses are called transoms.

## Answer:

*False. Men who wear dresses are called Shirley.*

## Answer true or false:

A condominium is a thing you use to keep from having babies.

## Answer:

*True.*

## Answer true or false:

When making love, you should always keep a bottle of rose water handy, just to sprinkle gently on your partner in case the fierce passion of your attack causes swooning from excitement.

## Answer:

*True, although gently sprinkling your partner with Yoo Hoo produces the same results.*

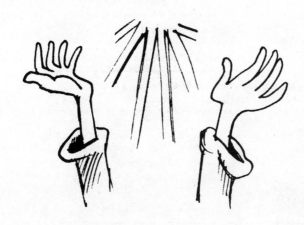

## Answer true or false:

When both partners have an orgasm at the same time, that's called "having an orgasm at the same time."

## Answer:

*False. When both partners have an orgasm at the same time, that's called "a miracle."*

# Test Your Sex IQ continued

## Choose one answer.

## Thighs are great because:

**1.** They keep your knees out of your groin.

**2.** They are the boulevard which leads to the avenue of love.

**3.** Without thighs there would not be laps, and without laps there would not be nude spanking.

*Answer: 3.* *Without thighs there would not be laps, and without laps there would not be nude spanking.*

## Choose one answer.

### When you come home and find satin sheets on the bed, it's a pretty good bet that:

**1.** The Pope is coming for a visit.

**2.** You are going to get your socks blown off.

**3.** You are in the wrong house.

*Answer: 3.* *You are in the wrong house.*

# TWICE IN ONE NIGHT

## YOU BET. HERE'S HOW.

Many people over 30 fondly remember the days when having sex three, four, five, even six times a night was not all that uncommon, and when their biggest problem was not getting stains on the magazine.

Now, some of those people are finding, the bloom is off the rose, the frost is on the pumpkin, and the old fastball has lost some of its zip, if you catch my drift. The ancient Greeks used to refer to this condition as "nuggied-out city."

"Oh," these over 30s despair, "is there any hope that I will ever be fulfilled twice in one night again?"

The answer is "of course," as long as you know how.

### How
Tie it to a broom.

These other humorous titles are available at fine bookstores or by sending $3.95 each plus $1.00 per book to cover postage and handling to the address below.

Please send me:

| QUAN. | | TITLE |
|---|---|---|
| | 5352-6 | Skinny People Are Dull and Crunchy Like Carrots |
| | 5370-4 | A Coloring Book for Pregnant Mothers to Be |
| | 5367-4 | Games You Can't Lose |
| | 5358-5 | The Trite Report |
| | 5357-7 | Happy Birthday Book |
| | 5356-9 | Adult Crossword Puzzles |
| | 5359-3 | Bridget's Workout Book |
| | 5360-7 | Picking Up Girls |
| | 5368-2 | Games for the John |
| | 5340-2 | Living in Sin |
| | 5341-0 | I Love You Even Tho' . . . |
| | 5342-9 | You Know You're Over 50 When . . . |
| | 5363-1 | You Know You're Over 40 When . . |
| | 5361-5 | Wimps |
| | 5354-2 | Sex Manual for People Over 30 |
| | 5353-4 | Small Busted Women Have Big Hearts |
| | 5369-0 | Games You Can Play with Your Pussy Cat (and Lots of Other Stuff Cat Owners Should Know) |
| | 5366-6 | Calories Don't Count If You Eat Standing Up |
| | 5365-8 | Do Diapers Give You Leprosy? What Every Parent Should Know About Bringing Up Babies |
| | 5355-0 | I'd Rather Be 40 Than Pregnant |
| | 5362-3 | Afterplay: How to Get Rid of Your Partner After Sex |

Send me _____ books at $3.95* each      $_____

Illinois residents add 8% sales tax; California residents add 6% sales tax:    _____

Add $1.00 per book for shipping/handling      _____

               **TOTAL $**_____

☐ Check or M.O. payable to Best Publications

Charge my    ☐ Visa    ☐ MasterCard

Acct. #_____ Exp. Date ____/____

X _____

Signature (required only if charging to Bankcard)

Name _____

Address _____

City/State/Zip _____

*Prices subject to change without notice.

Best Publications, Department IT
180 N. Michigan Ave., Chicago, IL 60601        BB 0784